# Count The
## DINOSAURS
# Book For Kids

# This Book Belongs To:

_____

# Count the dinosaurs!

# Congratulations! You guessed correctly

## There were 7

# DINOSAURS

# Find 2 of the same dinosaurs!

# Congratulations! You guessed correctly

## Here are 2 of the same

# DINOSAURS

# Count the flying dinosaurs!

# Congratulations! You guessed correctly

## There were 4 flying

# DINOSAURS

# Count the dinosaurs in the eggs!

# Congratulations! You guessed correctly

## There were 5

# DINOSAURS

## in the eggs

# Count the sleeping dinosaurs!

# Congratulations! You guessed correctly

## There were 2 sleeping

# DINOSAURS

# Count the dinosaurs!

# Congratulations! You guessed correctly

## There were 9

# DINOSAURS

# Find a flying dinosaur!

# Congratulations! You guessed correctly

## Here is the flying

# DINOSAUR

# Count the dinosaur eggs!

# Congratulations! You guessed correctly

## There were 11

# DINOSAUR

## eggs

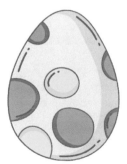

# Count the red dinosaurs!

# Congratulations! You guessed correctly

## There were 3 red

## DINOSAURS

# Count the dinosaurs with spots!

# Congratulations! You guessed correctly

## There were 4

# DINOSAURS

## with spots

# Count the spiked dinosaurs!

# Congratulations! You guessed correctly

## There was 1 spiked

# DINOSAUR

# Find 2 of the same dinosaurs!

# Congratulations! You guessed correctly

## Here are 2 of the same

# DINOSAURS

# Count the pink dinosaurs!

# Congratulations! You guessed correctly

## There were 5 pink

DINOSAURS

# Count the green dinosaurs!

# Congratulations! You guessed correctly

## There were 6 green

# DINOSAURS

# Are there more red or pink dinosaurs?

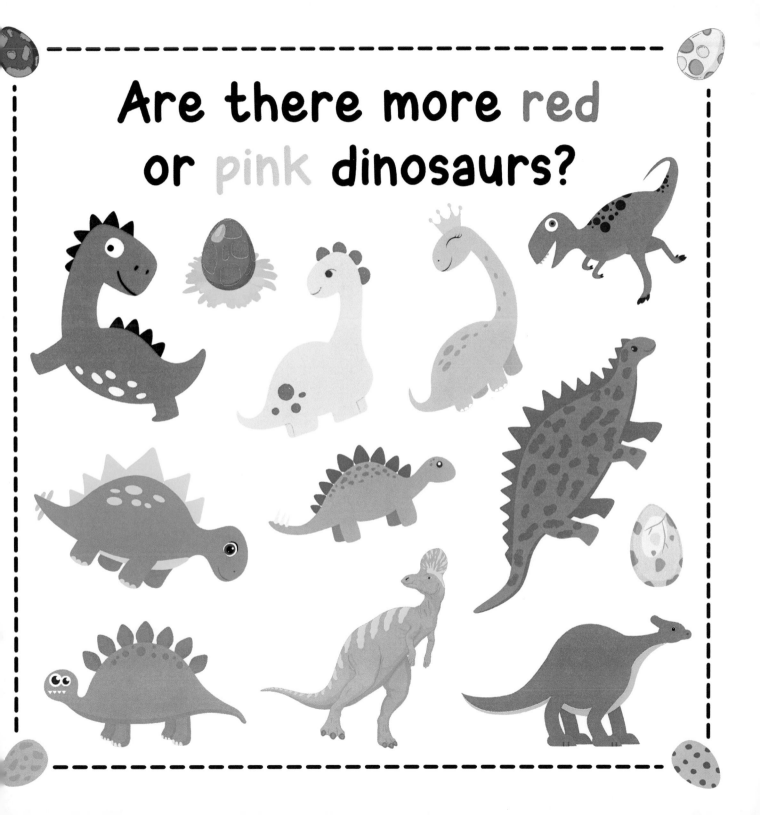

# Congratulations! You guessed correctly

## There were more red

**x3**

**x5**

# Count the dinosaur eggs!

# Congratulations! You guessed correctly

## There were 8

# DINOSAUR

## eggs

# Are there more eggs or dinosaurs?

# Congratulations! You guessed correctly

## There were more eggs

**x8**

**x7**

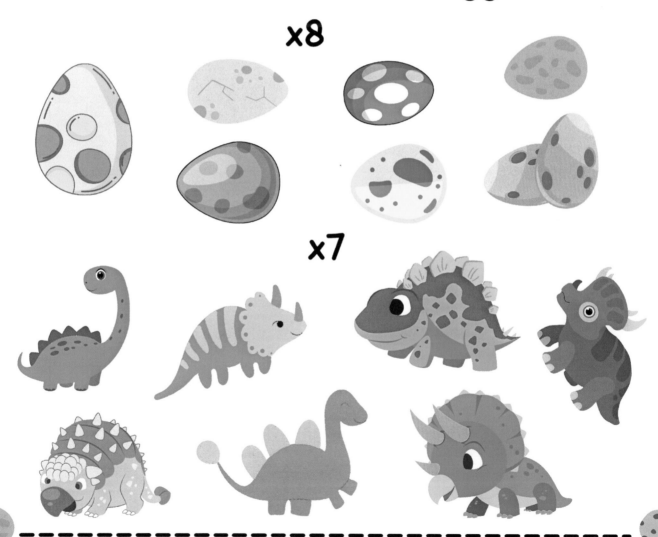

# Count the dinosaurs!

# Congratulations! You guessed correctly

## There were 10

# DINOSAURS

I AM VERY GRATEFUL YOU PURCHASED THIS BOOK. I HOPE YOU AND YOUR CHILD SPEND AN UNFORGETTABLE TIME HAVING FUN AND LEARNING TOGETHER FROM THIS BOOK.

IF YOU CAN, I WOULD BE EXTREMELY GRATEFUL IF YOU COULD LEAVE A REVIEW ON AMAZON. WE ARE A SMALL FAMILY BUSINESS AND DEPEND ON REVIEWS TO REACH MORE FAMILIES.

THANK YOU AGAIN FOR YOUR PURCHASE AND YOUR TRUST. I HOPE YOU ENJOY YOUR BOOK AND HAVE A GREAT TIME WITH YOUR FAMILY

WE HOPE THE BOOK HAS MET YOUR EXPECTATIONS, IF YOU FOUND ANY MISTAKES IN THE BOOK PLEASE CONTACT US BY EMAIL, AND WE WILL CORRECT THEM AS SOON AS POSSIBLE.

**office.dannyd@gmail.com**

**HAVE A NICE DAY !**

**INDEPENDENTLY PUBLISHED**

Carolin D. Lowe

Made in United States
North Haven, CT
04 November 2022

26224350R00022